Simple Sourdoughs

The Curious Peasant
Lost Skills in Cookery, Craft, and Culture

Victoria Osborne

Peasant Publishing
Wiltshire

ISBN-13: 978-1499388961
ISBN-10: 1499388969

Cover design by Ed Tolkien
Editor: Lisa Cussans

Text copyright Victoria Osborne 2014

Simple Sourdoughs

The Curious Peasant
Lost skills in cookery, craft, and culture

This book is copyright material and must not be copied, reproduced, transferred, distributed, leased, licensed or publicly performed or used in any way except as specially permitted in writing by the publishers, as allowed under the terms and conditions under which it was purchased or as strictly permitted by applicable copyright laws. Any unauthorised distribution or use of this text may be a direct infringement of the author's and publisher's rights and those responsible may be liable in law accordingly.

ISBN: 978-0-9929083-3-1

Version 1.0

Published by Peasant Publishing 2014

Victoria Osborne has asserted her right under the Copyright, Designs and Patents Act 1998 to be identified as the author of this work.

Table of Contents:

Frontispiece	1
Legal Notice	2
Table of Contents	3
Dedication	4
Why choose sourdough?	5
What is sourdough?	6
How to Make a starter	8
Maintaining your starter	12
Baking tips and techniques	13
How to make sourdough my way	16

The Recipes

Basic White Sourdough	26
Pain de Compagne	30
Linseedy Sourdough	34
Focaccia with Red Grapes and Fennel Seeds	38
Wholemeal or Wholewheat Sourdough	41
Sourdough Baguettes	44
Sourdough Pizza	49
Pretzels	52
Walnut and Raisin Bread	56
Prune and Pink Peppercorn Loaf	61
Borodinsky Bread	63
Sourdough with Mixed Seeds and Spelt	66
Crumpets	70
References	72
Glossary	73
Acknowledgements	74
Also by Victoria Osborne	75
About the Author	76
Did you like this book?	77

For Tim and Eleanor with love

Why choose sourdough?

Many people find the soft, pappy bread available in supermarkets to be very unsatisfying. Some have compared it to cotton wool, and, from a nutritional point of view, it may do you just about as much good. There are often complaints of indigestibility, too. Commercial white bread, for instance, gives me terrible heartburn and subsequent bloating, which I simply never get when eating a slowly fermented sourdough.

The consumption of rapidly made commercial bread pumped full of additives may go some way to explaining the extraordinary rise in perceived wheat intolerance in recent years. So many people these days are saying that bread doesn't "agree" with them, when frequently it is the commercially produced loaves so readily available that are the cause of the problem. On the other hand, a well-made, slowly fermented sourdough is usually a very satisfying, flavourful, and readily digested substance. The staff of life, indeed.

And keep in mind that with a homemade sourdough, the cook is in complete control of what goes into it. You can play with the recipe until you find a bread that suits your tastebuds, your pocket, and your diet. You can add walnuts, raisins, fruit, vegetables, or seeds. Have more or less salt (but you will need a little salt to help the gluten develop). You can make your bread with a variety of flours: brown, white, wholemeal, rye, barley, etc. Finally, making your own sourdough is not only very rewarding, but it can actually work out cheaper than buying bread commercially. Mind you, it is so delicious that you may well find yourselves eating rather a lot of it!

Unfortunately, most sourdoughs are not suitable to being made in a home bread maker. The mixing is too vigorous, and the proving time too short, for effective handling of the sourdough. However, if your bread maker machine has a "bake only" setting, you can experiment with placing your proved dough in the machine and seeing if the results are to your liking.

What is sourdough bread?

Most mass-produced commercial breads available in your local supermarket, particularly those bought from a baker or a supermarket in the United Kingdom, are made using the Chorleywood baking process. This is a method, developed in the early 1960s, of baking a light loaf of bread from a low protein flour in as short a time as possible. Industrial bakers have got this down to just a few short hours from the first mixing to the cooked loaf exiting the oven and being packaged ready for sale. The process uses lots of water, plenty of yeast, and a complex mixture of flour improvers, additives, preservatives, and enzymes, all of which help speed up the process and in turn reduce the cost. This also means that the grains in the flour have no opportunity to undergo a fermentation process. The result is a large, light, puffy, and pappy loaf. If you want to find out more about the contents and process of a Chorleywood loaf, I would recommend Andrew Whitley's superb book, Bread Matters.

A sourdough loaf, or at least my sourdough loaf, is the antithesis of the Chorleywood process. Natural yeast is "caught" in a mixture of flour and water. A wild yeast colony starts to grow, and, with judicious feeding and discarding, soon a vigorous starter mix is created. This is the sourdough culture, which is used in place of commercial yeast. This is, of course, the way bread has been made for millennia. Traditionally a bit of dough from an earlier baking was added to the current bake, in effect carrying over the natural yeast, just as in a sourdough starter but in a more solid form. Some good artisan bakers, particularly in Continental Europe, continue this practice. However, using dough from a previous bake is a little harder than cultivating a culture, which can live in the fridge for lengthy periods between bakes, and this book will concentrate on the more forgiving semi-liquid starter.

Making a sourdough loaf also takes time. As the natural yeast is slower growing than commercially produced dried or fresh yeast, it takes longer to develop in a dough mix. This additional time allows the dough to undergo a partial fermentation, which, in turn, makes the bread easier to digest as the gluten in the flour is transformed. Making a sourdough loaf, from the initial refreshment of the starter to cutting the cooled loaf, can take anything from 24 to 48 hours, depending on your methods and routine – all this will be explained further in the chapter on baking.

The slow development of the sourdough starter or culture, sometimes called a "mother," and of the dough itself, as well as fermenting the grain, effectively predigesting it, also allows lactic acids to develop, which gives a distinctive tang to the bread. Some people like this, others prefer a loaf with less of a sour tang. It is quite easy to control the amount of "sour" flavour, the flavour that gives sourdough its name – this will be discussed in the chapter on maintaining a starter. Lactic acid also helps to reduce the speed at which the glucose in the bread is released to the body, helping to avoid sugar highs and lows.

There is a theory that a specific locality has its own indigenous yeast that gives rise to a local flavour in a sourdough loaf, known as the "terroir" of a loaf. One example is San Francisco sourdough, said to have originated during the West Coast gold rush of the 1860s. Starter cultures brought to the area by gold prospectors gradually evolved until the distinctive San Francisco sourdough strain stabilised and can be identified by microbiologists today.

Sourdough bread is often made with a high hydration dough, that is with a high percentage of water in the mix. This gives loaf with an open texture, plenty of holes, quite a starchy crumb (the bread inside the loaf), and a full, satisfying flavour. The lack of added sugar in the loaf means that although it toasts exceptionally well it often doesn't brown well as toast – I find I have to put it through the toaster on the longest setting. The bread lasts well: a big loaf often lasts a full week, certainly making excellent toast towards the end of that period, and it makes wonderful croutons and breadcrumbs.

There is a move afoot among the baking community to rename sourdough, since it is thought the word "sour" puts people off trying the bread. Because of this you will see more and more bakers calling their sourdough "naturally raised" or some such equivalent name.

So to recap: what is sourdough? Bread made with naturally occurring yeast, cultivated in a starter, and then mixed into a slowly fermented dough using, for a straightforward loaf, nothing but flour, water, and salt.

How to make a starter

To make a starter to feed your sourdough requires very little effort, just time. Basically, a mixture of flour and water is left, loosely covered, in the open. It is stirred every day, with a little more flour and water being added daily. After a short period – sometimes two to three days, sometimes a week or more – the mixture should start bubbling gently. It is then ready to use.

Different flours can take longer to become an effective starter. A wheat flour starter can be a little slow to get going, so I always use rye flour begin with. Rye flour seems to be the most effective at "catching" and growing wild yeast. It is also the easiest starter to maintain, being very tolerant of a little neglect. I think it also adds an interesting flavour to a bread that could otherwise be made with just white flour.

Some people swear by introducing substances that are neither flour nor water in the hope of introducing wild yeast to the culture more quickly – a small bunch of red grapes, for instance. I have never really found this to be an effective method, not least because the yeast found on grape skins, while fantastic for making wine, are not the yeast you need for making bread. Likewise, it has been suggested that water straight out of the tap contains too many impurities and additives to allow the yeast to grow. While it is true that water in many areas is chlorinated and bleach will kill yeast, the levels are usually low enough to be ignored. I always use tap water to make my starters, but, if you have very high levels of chlorine in your water, you might consider using bottled mineral water instead.

You will need:

A deep bowl or two, preferably transparent
A wooden spoon, or a whisk
A plastic dough scraper, or a silicone spoon
A clean tea towel or dish cloth
Rye flour
Water

Day 1:

In a deep bowl, thoroughly mix 150g rye flour with 150ml tepid water. Give this a vigorous whisking to incorporate some air. Clean down the sides of the bowl using a dough scraper or a silicone spoon so that all the mixture is in the base with no bits drying out on the edge of the bowl. Alternatively, decant the mixture into a clean bowl. Drape the bowl with the clean tea towel or dish cloth and leave in a draught-free place.
Day 2, AM:

Add 150g rye flour and another 150ml tepid water to the mixture in the bowl. Give this another vigorous stir. Again, clean the sides of the bowl or decant into a clean bowl. Drape the bowl with the clean tea towel or dish cloth and leave in a draught-free place.

Day 2, PM:

Stir the mix and clean the bowl. Cover with the tea towel or dish cloth

Day 3, AM:

You may begin to see a little activity in the mix. Small craters or holes start appearing on the surface and you should see structural changes in the mix itself if you put a spoon in it. You will start to notice a difference in the smell: it may become slightly sour, yeasty, and have a vaguely alcoholic aroma. These are all signs that the yeast is multiplying. However, it may take a few more days before this stage is reached. Add 150g rye flour and another 150ml tepid water. Repeat the actions of Day 2 AM.

Day 3, PM:

Stir the mix and clean the bowl. Cover with the tea towel or dish cloth.

Day 4, AM:

Check for activity. By now you will have quite a large quantity of mix so you will have to either throw or give some of it away. A pity, but it's all part of the process. Alternatively, you could make some crumpets from the last recipe in this book. Discard half the mixture, add your now-familiar 150g flour and the 150ml water, and stir well. Clean the bowl and cover with a tea towel or dish cloth.

Day 4, PM:

Stir the mix and clean the bowl. Cover with the tea towel or dish cloth. If your starter has picked up some wild yeast and the colony has started to grow, you will notice that soon after adding the new flour the mix will "rise" or "heave" up the inside of the bowl, and then fall back again. This is why a transparent bowl is so useful, since you will be able to see when the mix has risen.

Continue this process of stirring, discarding, and feeding until your starter is looking very healthy, smells nice, and is active after feeding. Some starters become very active and will even overflow the bowl. Others are more sluggish. Continue to look after it daily, and it will slowly become more active. When your starter is active you can cover it with cling film or plastic wrap and put it in the fridge until you need it. On one occasion, I left mine for four weeks and I still was able to use it after a little cosseting.

I prefer to use a starter which is approximately equal quantities of flour and water. This gives a thick sludgy mix reminiscent of porridge. Some like to have the starter a little thicker – it is your personal choice, whichever is easiest for you to work with. Just remember to slightly adjust the quantities of water in your dough mix to make up for it. If your starter regularly and rapidly separates into a sludgy mix beneath a grayish black thin liquid, stir this back into the mix and slightly increase the quantity of flour to water when you feed it.

If after all the feeding and stirring nothing has happened to your young starter mix, and it is showing no signs of life after several days or a week, then discard the mix and start again.

Check all your bowls and implements are clean with no soap residues. Make sure your clean tea towel or dish cloth is not impregnated with powerful aromas from washing powder, which might inhibit the growth of the wild yeast. Consider using bottled water or water that has been boiled and allowed to cool in place of ordinary tap water. Finally, check to see that your flour is fresh and well within its use-by date.

Persevere and your starter will come to life.

How to maintain a starter and refresh it for baking

Once you have a vigorous and healthy starter, you need to look after it. A well-fed and maintained starter will not only allow you to bake daily or weekly but, barring tragedies, it will also last a lifetime – mine is over five years old. You will also be able, instead of discarding the starter, to give some to your friends so they, too, can begin to bake their own loaves.

Twelve hours before you plan to bake, take your starter out of the fridge. It may have separated into a layer of liquid and a layer of sludge, so give it a good stir. Stir it even if it hasn't separated. Throw half your starter away, and then add an equal quantity of rye flour and tepid water to what remains in the bowl. Give it another good stir. Clean the bowl or decant the mix into a clean bowl, cover loosely with cling film or plastic wrap, and leave out on the kitchen worktop.

When you are ready to bake, take out and keep to one side the quantity of starter you need for your chosen recipe. Add more flour and water to the starter you are keeping for your next bake, stir well, clean the bowl, cover with cling film or plastic wrap, and return the bowl to the fridge for next time. The starter you want to bake with should have been refreshed at least once about 12 hours before baking.

I have left a starter untended in my fridge for as long as four weeks. It looks pretty horrid at the end of this time, a deep layer of blackish liquid over a grayish sludge, and it can smell very sour indeed. Don't worry, just feed and refresh it several times at regular intervals, discarding half your mix each time you refresh it, and it will soon come back to life.

Some people freeze a quantity of starter and revive it with feeding after it has defrosted. I have never tried this as I bake very regularly and have never had to leave the starter longer than about four weeks, but it might be worth experimenting with. Certainly fresh yeast freezes well, although it goes a bit slimy when defrosted, so there is no reason why the wild yeast in a vigorous starter shouldn't survive a period in the freezer.

A word of warning: never store your starter in a sealed glass jar. The continuing activity of the yeast in the starter will give off CO_2 as a bi-product. Even in the cool atmosphere of the fridge this process continues, and there is a risk of the carbon dioxide build-up being so great as to explode the jar. Play it safe and, if you are using a glass vessel, cover it with cling film or plastic wrap. This will keep out contaminants but still allow the CO_2 to escape.

Before you bake

Useful tips and techniques

There is no doubt about it: dough is sticky. You can guarantee that as soon as both hands are in a bowl of dough working the mass of flour, yeast, and water into a cohesive whole, that's the moment the telephone will ring, your sleeves will slip down over your wrists, or your specs will slither down your nose. The only way to cope is to be organised and try to keep one hand out of the mix. This is where the plastic dough scraper or "bread flap" comes in so handy. You can hold this in your working hand and rotate the bowl with the other. Scrape the mix down the sides of the bowl, and use it to lift and fold the half-mixed mess into the centre of the bowl until everything is incorporated. This keeps at least one hand clean for emergencies. I usually keep two bread flaps in play – one to scrape and manipulate the mix and the other to periodically scrape the working hand clean again. As for the slipping sleeves problem: I often long for those elasticated straps sported by telegraph operators in old cowboy movies, they would keep your sleevies up. Despite numerous folds and pushing up above the elbows, sleeves have an extraordinary habit of lengthening, slithering down again, and becoming an infernal nuisance. Baking is warm work, however, and short sleeves will probably be more comfortable, even in cool weather.

For the initial mixing of both the starter and the dough, I like to use the handle of a wooden spoon. This does the job well and is easy to scrape clean. When the dough is partially mixed, I move onto the plastic dough scraper.

Salt has been receiving a very bad press, and there might be a temptation to try and bake without it. It is true that the Tuscans often make a bread without salt, and it is also true that your palette becomes used to low salt levels. However, a little salt in bread is necessary, not just for the savour and flavour but also because it affects the way the glutens in the flour take up water. So by all means reduce the salt levels in the recipes that follow, but don't cut out all the salt completely. One further word about salt. Yeast and salt do not get on; in fact, salt in concentration will kill yeast. Try always to have a buffer of flour between the starter mix and salt you add – either mix the flour and salt together before adding it to the water and starter, add the salt after the flour, or even add the salt after you have done the initial mixing. If you choose this latter course you must make sure it is well mixed in, so you may have to do a little traditional kneading to ensure it is evenly distributed.

While the dough is proving in bowls, it needs to be covered. I recommend using cling film or plastic wrap as most people have this in their kitchens. However, the disposable shower caps that you sometimes find in hotel rooms are incredibly useful here. Cling film or plastic wrap, if you can get it off the roll, often won't stick to plastic bowls (wet the rims slightly and it will) or it sticks firmly to itself. The transparent shower caps have an elasticated rim and are perfect for the job of covering a mixing bowl. You can see through them, and so keep an eye on your dough. They fit perfectly, don't stick to themselves, and, although flimsy, if they are treated kindly, they will last for several bakes. I like them so much that I bought a large quantity on eBay so that I am never likely to run out!

Once your dough is mixed, proved, scaled (baker's speak for weighed), and moulded, you then have to clean all your bowls. It is no use trying to wash up with hot water and a washing-up brush. The starches in the flour will immediately turn to gluey lumps and gum everything up. Likewise if you try to use a washing-up sponge or mop. Everything becomes glued up with a substance that resembles soft chewing gum. The most successful method is to use one of those cheap plastic doughnut-shaped scourers with cool or tepid water. The soggy mess accumulates in the holes in the plastic scourer and can easily be picked out. The dough residues in bowls dissolve and can be washed away, the bowl then being rinsed with hotter water and left to drain.

I tend not to wash my baking tins at all, unless something has stuck badly. Before each use they are oiled and floured, and after the bread has been removed from the tins they are allowed to cool and then put away. Eventually a wonderfully seasoned surface will build up, and less preparation of the tins will be needed before baking.

How to make sourdough my way

The stages in baking yeasted bread are quite simple but some of the techniques used in making a sourdough my way are a little unfamiliar and gentler than you might expect. My method requires almost no kneading and no knocking back, for instance.

Commonly used method for bread making	My method for sourdough
Mix flour, water, salt and yeast	Refresh starter
Knead	Mix flour, water, salt and starter
Prove	Autolyse
Knock Back	Turn and fold x 4
Mould and shape	Mould and shape
Prove	Prove
Bake	Bake
Cool	Cool
Eat	Eat

First, refresh your starter by discarding half your stored starter and adding flour and water. Mix well and leave to become active by the process known as "autolyse".

Measure your ingredients and mix thoroughly – I like to use electronic scales that I can reset to zero between adding ingredients. First I weigh my water, reset the scales to zero, and then add the required amount of starter, stirring gently to disperse it. Reset the scales to zero again, add the flour, then the salt. Mix the ingredients until they are well amalgamated, scrape the inside of the bowl clean, cover with a clean tea towel or dish cloth, and leave it for 10 minutes to half an hour. This pre-soaking process known as "autolyse" allows the flour to absorb the water and starts the development of the gluten in the flour. At this stage I take the opportunity to top up or refresh my reserved starter mix, cover and return it to the fridge, and to clean up my work area.

After the initial period of autolyse the dough needs turning and folding. Uncover the bowl and take a handful of the dough farthest from you. Gently stretch it away from the mass of the dough and then fold it back towards yourself, over the top of the dough. Rotate the bowl a quarter turn and repeat this stretching and folding four times, until the whole mass of dough has been stretched and folded over itself. Imagine the back of an envelope and use that as the basis for the stretching and folding – each side of the dough mix being one flap of the envelope.

Cover the bowl with the tea towel or dish cloth, and leave it another half hour.

Repeat this stretching and folding four times at half-hourly intervals. It should take no more than a minute or two each time. As you do it you will see how the dough is changing in character. The first stretch and fold is with a gloopy mass of dough. By the second stretch and fold the dough has undergone an extraordinary transformation and become dough. By the fourth stretch and fold you should have a slightly shiny, stretchy, puffy mass of sweet-smelling dough.

At this stage you need to prepare your moulds or baking tins.

For a free-form loaf, either a round or oval shape, you need to have a mould, something the proving loaf can rest in that helps it retain its shape. I use a variety of moulds, from purpose-made bannetone baskets to enamel pie dishes, cheap willow or rattan baskets, bowls and plastic colanders. Anything that is the right size and shape. These need to be lined with a linen baking cloth that has been liberally dusted with flour. You can buy very expensive linen-lined baskets, but I am happy using half a linen tea towel or dish cloth in whatever mould comes to hand.

If you want to make a tin loaf then lightly oil or grease the inside of the tin and dust it with flour.

Shaping and moulding your bread

After the fourth rest you can shape your dough. Using a plastic bread scraper, gently encourage your dough mix out of the bowl and onto a lightly oiled work surface. Try not to expel the air – this is a crucial difference from standard bread making, which requires you to "knock back" all the air from your proved dough. For sourdough you want to retain as much of this air as possible. Using a palette knife, a dough knife, or the edge of your plastic bread scraper, cut the dough into the required size. For instance, if I am using a kilo of flour I would cut this into two equal-sized pieces. Since I sell my bread I always weigh my dough pieces so that each loaf is the same size as the next, but this is not strictly necessary for home baking.

Gently repeat the stretching, folding, and rotating technique so the four edges of the dough are pulled over the centre. This has the effect of gently tightening the under-surface of the dough. While doing this final stretch and fold you need to consider the final shape of your bread. If you are making a free-form round loaf or "boule," try to make the dough fairly round. If an oval or a tin loaf is wanted, then make your stretch and fold more rectangular. The final shaping of your loaf is designed to create a lovely, smooth, and taut upper surface with the folded seam below.

For a round loaf, turn the loaf over so the upper smooth surface is on top and, using both hands, rotate the loaf while tucking the side of your hand below the underside, gently pulling and tightening the dough and creating a smooth upper surface and a neat round shape as you do so. If this surface starts to tear, you are pulling too hard; just allow the dough to relax for a few minutes and then try tightening it a little again. Don't worry too much about a few surface tears, they often disappear in the baking. If you are using a mould for your round loaf then turn the loaf over again so the seam is uppermost, and place the dough into the mould smooth-side down. Gently pinch the seam together, sprinkle the surface with flour, and fold the surplus bits of cloth gently over the dough. Place the mould in a draught-free spot, and lightly cover with a piece of plastic. The bags magazines are posted in are useful here; opened lengthwise, one envelope can cover a couple of baskets. Leave to prove again.

For an oval free-form loaf, take your rough rectangle of dough with both hands and place your thumbs in the centre of the dough while your fingers roll the dough over your thumbs, making a cylindrical shape, at the same time trying to pull and tighten the loaf surface. Place in your prepared, lined, and floured mould, smooth-side down. Pinch the seam together, lightly flour the surface, and fold the excess cloth over the top. Place the mould in a draught-free location, and lightly cover the upper surface with a piece of plastic.

Covering the baskets with a light layer of plastic helps prevent the surface of the dough drying out and the formation of a skin, which might inhibit the rise of the bread in the oven.

If you are making tin loaves, use the same shaping techniques described above but place the formed dough into the prepared tins seam-side down. Again, cover with clean cloth and a light layer of plastic.

It is possible to put the loaves into the fridge as soon as you have put them in the moulds or tins, which will slow down or retard the final rise. This allows you to fit the baking into your own timetable, for instance if you mix and shape your dough in the afternoon and want to bake the following day. If you do this, be sure to let the loaves come back to room temperature before baking. The dough can also become a little damp if it has spent time in the fridge. If this is the case, leave the loaves uncovered while they are returning to room temperature so the surface can dry out. Note that cold retardation can increase the sour flavour of your bread, so this strategy might not suit if you like a milder-flavoured loaf.

The formed dough will now take anywhere from 2-6 hours to be ready for baking. My kitchen has a fairly consistent temperature, and my loaves usually take about 3-4 hours. Your dough is ready for baking when it is noticeably larger than when you put it in the moulds or tins, and if you gently press the back of a finger against the dough, the impression it makes should remain. If you try this test at intervals you will be able to tell more easily as the younger, unrisen, dough will spring back much more readily.

Slashing the loaves

When bread dough is placed into a hot oven the carbon dioxide in the loaf expands rapidly, making most loaves rise dramatically and often tearing the surface of the loaf in the process. This tearing can be encouraged and controlled by slashing or scoring the tops of the loaves. A very sharp knife, a razor blade, scissors, or a baker's "lame" can all be used. A firm, fast slash gives the best results. Sometimes wetting the blade will prevent it dragging at the dough. If you just want a single cut with a pronounced "lift" or tear on the surface of the loaf, then cut at an angle of about 30 degrees to the surface. If you want a pattern of cuts as an identifying mark for each different style of loaf, then make your cuts vertical to the surface. Traditionally, loaves taken to a communal bake oven would have been identified in this way, with each baker using their own style of cut.

Baking

Bread needs to be cooked in a very hot, preferably slightly moist, oven, and there are various ways to achieve this.

Baking in a Dutch oven or casserole:

You can bake your free-form loaves in a Dutch oven or large lidded casserole dish. The Dutch oven or casserole needs to be preheated in a hot oven. When the loaf is ready to bake, the pan is taken out of the oven, the lid removed, the loaf carefully turned out of its mould and slipped into the pan, the top of the loaf slashed, the pan lid put on, and the pan returned to the oven. This creates a hot, steamy space in which the loaf will rise magnificently. After 20 minutes the lid of the pan is removed and the loaf allowed to finish cooking and for the crust to brown. This method works incredibly well, giving a lot of "oven spring," where the loaf rises fast in the first 15 minutes of baking. The steam given off by the loaf is trapped in the pan and encourages this rise. The disadvantages are having to use a very big and possibly heavy casserole dish, plus it is all too easy to burn yourself on the very hot pan both when you are putting the loaf in and when you are slashing the top.

Baking in a ceramic baking dome:

You can buy a purpose-made ceramic baking dome: La Cloche for instance, is a great product but expensive, and there are others on the market. This has the same effect as the Dutch oven, trapping the steam and encouraging good oven spring. It is perhaps a little easier to use than the Dutch oven as the dome has a handle on the top and the edges of the base are low, so the risk of burns is somewhat reduced. The La Cloche domes are object of beauty but perhaps too pricey for the peasant.

Using a baking stone and inverted saucepan:

I often use a baking stone with a large saucepan inverted over it. Preheat your stone and saucepan in your oven. The bread is placed onto the edge of a rimless baking sheet (I use the underside of a lipped sheet) that has been liberally dusted with semolina. This is the equivalent of the long-handled bread "peel" that commercial bakers use. I open the oven door and with one hand (in an oven glove) I raise the inverted hot pan while with the other hand I introduce the bread into the oven. Place the baking sheet where you want your loaf of bread to sit, angle it slightly upwards, and give a sharp jerk away from the loaf. The loaf should slide sweetly off and sit on the hot baking stone. Carefully lower the hot saucepan back over the loaf and shut the oven door. Again this acts like a Dutch oven and traps the steam that escapes from the baking loaf. For a baking stone you can either use a commercial pizza stone or an unglazed terracotta floor tile. The saucepan is removed after about 20 minutes of baking.

Baking bread in a bread tin:

The most common method of home baking is in bread tins that are simply placed on the hot oven rack. The only difference I would suggest is to place an empty baking tray to preheat under the lowest rack of the oven. Then, after the tins have been put in the oven, quickly pour a little water into the baking tray and shut the oven door. This introduces some steam into the oven, thereby helping the loaves to rise. I usually add a little more water after about 10 minutes. Be careful introducing the water. You don't want to splash it about as you run the risk of hitting the bulb in your oven light, the element, and the glass door. All to be avoided!

Is the bread cooked?

If your bread is cooked in a hot enough oven then it should, depending on the size of loaf, cook through in about 30-40 minutes. You can test for "doneness" by using a catering thermometer. The internal temperature of a cooked loaf should be about 190°C or 375°F. An enriched loaf, one made with added eggs, oil or butter, should be a little higher, at about 200°C or 390°F. However, using a thermometer makes a hole in your loaf through which steam can escape, something I try to avoid as the loaf continues to cook as it cools and needs its internal steam to finish this process.

Another method to tell if your loaf is cooked is to take it out of the oven and tap it firmly under the base with the fingers of one hand while holding it in the other hand. You should be able to feel a hollow vibration throughout the loaf if it is done. This technique takes a bit of time to get the hang of, and many people just say that when you get a "hollow" sound the loaf is done. It is worth persevering with trying to feel the vibration of the done loaf as it is a slightly better indicator of doneness than the sound alone.

As to crust colour – the darker the crust, the greater the flavour. I tend to leave my sourdough loaves in the oven a little longer than some others might as the increased crust texture and flavour of a well-done loaf enhances my pleasure in eating it. However, if you prefer a paler crust then take your loaves out of the oven as soon as you think they are cooked. If they are browning too quickly for your taste, drape a piece of baking parchment or greaseproof paper over them to slow the browning down.

Allow to cool

As soon as your loaf is cooked, take it out of the oven – and its tin if you are using tins – and place it on a rack to cool. The temptation to cut into your hot loaf is great, but the internal texture of the loaf will be greatly improved if you can resist cutting too soon. Try and leave it at least an hour. The steam inside the loaf is continuing to cook the crumb, and the starches are still setting. As the bread cools you will hear it "singing" – an unexpected and delightful aspect of making your own sourdoughs

This may seem a fairly daunting schedule for making a loaf of bread, but please don't be put off. The actually work time is about 10 minutes in total, with maybe 40 minutes baking. There are a lot of intervals when nothing is happening except the yeast working its magic with the dough.

You will find these instructions repeated within each recipe, since it's easier than having to flip back to these instructions each time you need a reminder.

A note about weights and measures

In Great Britain we have now almost completely converted to the metric system of weights and measures, and many professional cooks in the USA are now using metric weights, too. All my recipes are made using metric weights, in part because it is so easy to scale up a metric recipe, and in part because it is what I am used to. If you are using an electronic scale, which I recommend, you can usually switch the mode of weighing between grams and millilitres and pounds and ounces. I am sorry, too, if you are disappointed not to find "cup" measurements. I have always found the weighing of dry goods by cup to be a bit hit and miss. If your flour, for instance, is spooned into a measure which is then tapped on the worktop to level it off, it may well end up weighing more than a measure of flour which is filled by spoon, held in a hand and not tapped to level it off. There are good weight to cup conversion tables on the internet so if you prefer to cook with cup measurements it would be worth trying them out. Finally, very small quantities are given in spoon measures. It can often be quicker and simpler to add a spoonful of something than to weigh out very small amounts. Sticky things too, like molasses and malt syrup, are easier to handle using spoons. If you keep you spoon in a cup of boiling or very hot water the sticky stuff is even easier to handle.

The Recipes – Basic White Sourdough

This recipe makes the most straightforward loaf of bread. This is my everyday staple and a bestseller for my bread business. It is made using a two-stage overnight process. Some flour, water, and the starter are mixed together in the evening, making a "sponge" or "poolish." The following morning the rest of the flour is added, together with salt, and the bread is made.

1125g stoneground white flour
650ml water
175g rye sourdough starter (a large ladleful)
25g fine sea salt

Using an electronic scale that you can reset to zero, weigh out 650ml tepid water. Reset the scales to zero and add 175g vigorous rye sourdough starter. Mix gently to disperse the starter in the water. Reset the scales to zero again and add 500g of the flour. Stir thoroughly, clean the insides of the bowl or decant the mix into a clean bowl, cover with cling film or plastic wrap and leave overnight. This sloppy mix may start working straight away and you will see the first small holes and craters in the surface even as you are covering it.

The next morning you will see that the surface of your sloppy mix has bubbles all over it, a sure sign that the yeast is multiplying. Add the remaining 625g flour to the mix, put in the salt, and mix thoroughly. This stage is quite hard work as the poolish is often reluctant to take all the extra flour. However, persevere for a couple of minutes and the mix will come roughly together. At this stage, scrape down the insides of the bowl, cover it, and leave it for 10-30 minutes. This short period of autolyse will allow the new flour to start absorbing the liquid in the mix and make it easier to complete the mixing process.

Uncover the bowl and, using the plastic bread scraper or your hand, follow the stretch and fold technique outlined earlier and stretch and fold the contents of the bowl for two full rotations, that is eight stretches and folds. Again scrape the inside of the bowl clean and cover with cling film or plastic wrap.

Repeat this stretch and fold at half-hourly intervals for two hours, four times in total. You don't need eight stretches and folds after the original time though, four times will be adequate. You will notice each time you turn the dough that it is transforming its character, becoming more dough-like.

Half an hour after the fourth turning, gently ease the now puffy dough onto a lightly oiled work surface. Stretch and fold the dough to make a neat shape, either round or rectangular, and then complete your moulding to the shape you prefer. For a round loaf put the seam-side down and, using the side of your hand, rotate the loaf gently, pulling the sides under the base and tightening the surface. For an oval loaf, using your thumbs, roll the dough up into a tight cylinder shape.

Place the dough in your chosen moulds, lined with rye flour-dusted cloths, seam-side up. Pinch the seam closed, dust with a little more rye flour, and gently fold the spare cloth over the top of the dough. Leave in a draught-free spot to prove, and cover with a sheet of plastic. Alternatively, put the dough into oiled and floured tins, seam-side down.

The dough will take between 2-6 hours to prove. Test it periodically with the back of a finger to see when it is ready to bake. A dent will spring back quickly while the bread is still proving; this becomes slower as it reaches optimum proof.

Your oven should be preheated to a hot setting, 240°C/475°F/Gas Mark 9. If using a Dutch oven or a baking stone, these should also be preheated. Don't forget to put an empty baking tray in the bottom of the oven if you are baking your loaves uncovered or in tins.

For baking a free-form loaf in a Dutch oven:

Take out the preheated Dutch oven and remove its lid. Gently tip the dough out of its mould onto your hand and carefully lay it, seam-side down, in the bottom of the Dutch oven. Take a knife and slash the top of the loaf in the pattern your prefer – be careful, it is at this point that it is very easy to burn yourself on the sides of the very hot pan. Quickly place the lid back on the pan and pop it back in the oven. After 20 minutes, remove the lid of the Dutch oven to allow the now well-risen loaf to continue cooking and brown the crust. After another 15-20 minutes, test the loaf for doneness by tapping it underneath, listening for the hollow sound, and feeling the vibration of a done loaf. If cooked, put it on a wire rack to cool. If more time is needed, return it to the oven until done.

For baking a free-form loaf on a stone under a pan:

Preheat your baking stone and a large inverted pan on top of it. Generously dust the rimless underside of a baking sheet with semolina. Carefully un-mould your dough, seam-side down, onto the edge of the baking sheet. Slash the top of the dough in your preferred pattern. Open the oven and, using a glove, lift the nearest edge of the very hot pan. With the other hand place the edge of the baking sheet with the dough on it in the position you want the bread to settle in the oven. Tilt the nearest edge of the baking sheet up a little and give a sharp jerk back towards you. The dough should slip sweetly off the baking sheet and sit on the baking stone. Carefully lower the hot saucepan back down over the dough, making sure you don't squash its edges, and shut the oven door. After 20 minutes, check the bread. If it is well risen, remove the saucepan to allow the bread to continue cooking. After another 15-20 minutes, test the loaf for doneness by tapping it underneath, listening for the hollow sound and feeling the vibration of a done loaf. If cooked, put it on a wire rack to cool. If more time is needed, return it to the oven until done.

For baking a loaf in a bread tin:

Place a baking tray in the bottom of your oven and allow it to preheat. When your bread is ready to bake, slash the top in your preferred pattern and gently place the tin on the oven rack. Pour a little water into the hot baking tray at the bottom of the oven, then quickly shut the oven door. After 10 minutes, open the door and pour a little more water into the baking tray. Shut the door again. Reduce the oven temperature a little to 220°C/425°F/Gas Mark 7. Keep an eye on the bread and after 30-40 minutes test for doneness. Take your loaf out of the oven and tip it out of the tin, tapping it on the underside. There should be a hollow sound and you may feel a vibration through the loaf. If the bread needs a little longer it can go back in the oven out of the tin, straight onto the oven rack. When cooked, the loaf should be removed from its tin, if still in it, and placed on a wire rack to cool.

Pain de Compagne

Using half wholemeal flour and half white flour, this recipe makes a classic rustic French loaf with a great crust and a fantastic flavour. The proportion of wholemeal makes the loaf a little denser than the white sourdough, but the overnight soaking of the wholemeal flour helps the rise considerably.

490g stoneground wholemeal flour
490g stoneground white flour
275g young vigorous rye starter
610ml tepid water
20g salt

The evening before you want to bake, weigh out the tepid water on a pair of electronic scales, reset the scales to zero, and add the refreshed rye starter. Stir gently to disperse. Reset the scales to zero again and add the wholemeal flour. Mix well, clean the insides of the bowl, cover with cling film or plastic wrap, and leave the sloppy mix in a draught-free place overnight.

The next morning you will see that the surface of your sloppy mix has bubbles all over it, a sure sign that the yeast is multiplying. Add the white flour and the salt, and mix thoroughly. This stage is quite hard work as the poolish is often reluctant to take all the extra flour. However, persevere for a couple of minutes and the mix will come roughly together. Now scrape down the insides of the bowl, cover it, and leave it for 10-30 minutes. This short period of autolyse will allow the new flour to start absorbing the liquid in the mix and make it easier to complete the mixing process.

Uncover the bowl and, using the plastic bread scraper or your hand, follow the stretch and fold technique outlined earlier. Stretch and fold the contents of the bowl for two full rotations, that is eight stretches and folds. Again scrape the inside of the bowl clean and cover with plastic.

Repeat this stretch and fold at half-hourly intervals for two hours, four times in total. You don't need eight stretches and folds after the initial time though, four times will be enough. You will notice that each time you turn the dough it is transforming its character, becoming more dough-like.

Half an hour after the fourth turning, gently ease the now puffy dough onto a lightly oiled work surface. Stretch and fold the dough to make a neat shape, either round or rectangular, and then complete your moulding to the shape you prefer. For a round loaf put the seam-side down and using the side of your hand rotate the loaf gently, pulling the sides under the base and thereby tightening the surface. For an oval loaf, using your thumbs, roll the dough up into a tight cylinder shape.

Place the dough in your chosen moulds, lined with rye flour-dusted cloths, seam-side up. Pinch the seam closed, dust with a little more rye flour, and gently fold the spare cloth over the top of the dough. Put in a draught-free spot to prove, and cover with a sheet of plastic. Alternatively, put the dough into oiled and floured tins, seam-side down.

The dough will take between 2-6 hours to prove. Test it periodically with the back of a finger to see when it is ready to bake. A dent will spring back quickly while the bread is still proving, becoming slower as it reaches optimum proof.

Your oven should be preheated to a hot setting, 240°C/475°F/Gas Mark 9. If using a Dutch oven or a baking stone, these should also be preheated. Don't forget to put an empty baking tray in the bottom of the oven if you are baking your loaves uncovered or in tins.

For baking a free-form loaf in a Dutch oven:

Take the preheated Dutch oven and remove its lid. Gently tip the dough out of its mould onto your hand and carefully lay it, seam-side down, in the bottom of the Dutch oven. Take a knife and slash the top of the loaf in the pattern your prefer – be careful, it is at this point that it is very easy to burn yourself on the sides of the very hot pan. Quickly place the lid back on the pan and pop it back in the oven. After 20 minutes, remove the lid of the Dutch oven to allow the now well-risen loaf to continue cooking and brown the crust. After another 15-20 minutes, test the loaf for doneness by tapping it underneath, listening for the hollow sound and feeling the vibration of a done loaf. If cooked, put it on a wire rack to cool. If more time is needed, return it to the oven until done.

For baking a free-form loaf on a stone under a pan:

Preheat your baking stone and a large inverted pan on top of it. Generously dust the flat underside of a baking sheet with semolina. Carefully un mould your dough, seam-side down, onto the edge of the baking sheet. Slash the top of the dough in your preferred pattern. Open the oven and, using a glove, lift the nearest edge of the very hot pan. With the other hand place the edge of the baking sheet with the dough on it in the position you want the bread in the oven. Tilt the nearest edge of the baking sheet up a little, and give a sharp jerk back towards you. The dough should slip sweetly off the baking sheet and sit on the baking stone. Carefully lower the hot saucepan back down over the dough, making sure you don't squash its edges, and shut the oven door. After 20 minutes, check the bread. If it is well risen, remove the saucepan to allow the bread to continue cooking. After another 15-20 minutes, test the loaf for doneness by tapping it underneath, listening for the hollow sound and feeling the vibration of a done loaf. If cooked, put it on a wire rack to cool. If more time is needed, return it to the oven until done.

For baking a loaf in a bread tin:

Place a baking tray in the bottom of your oven and allow it to preheat. When your bread in its tin is ready to bake, slash the top in your preferred pattern and gently place the tin on the oven rack. Pour a little water into the hot baking tray at the bottom of the oven, then quickly shut the oven door. After 10 minutes, open the door and pour a little more water into the baking tray. Shut the door again. Reduce the oven temperature a little to 220°C/425°F/Gas Mark 7. Keep an eye on your loaf, and after 30-40 minutes test it for doneness. Remove from the oven and tip it out of the tin, tapping it on the underside. There should be a hollow sound and you may feel a vibration through the loaf. If the bread needs a little longer it can go back in the oven out of the tin, straight onto the oven rack. When cooked it should be removed from the tin, if still in it, and placed on a wire rack to cool.

Linseedy Sourdough

This recipe uses the seeded bread flour that is readily obtainable in most supermarkets. It is a mix of wheat flour, wheat flakes, malt flour, and a variety of seeds, often including sunflower, pumpkin, oats, and linseeds. I like to add extra linseeds, and I make this with my sourdough starter instead of yeast. This produces a fairly dense but very flavoursome loaf. It toasts beautifully, but be careful not to burn it as the sugars from the malt flour allow it to burn easily.

These bags of flour are usually sold in 1kg weights, and one bag will give you two good-sized loaves (about 600g each).

This is a very easy recipe with almost no kneading, but it does require overnight soaking and the extra linseeds should also be soaked and then added in the morning. I usually start my mix just before going to bed but you can, of course, adapt the timings to suit yourself.

You will need a hot oven, 240°C/475°F/Gas Mark 9, and a baking tray placed under the lowest oven rack so you can add some water to create steam.

1kg malted grain flour
330ml water
350g rye starter (two big ladlesful)
50g linseeds
Boiling water to soak the linseeds
15g fine sea salt

Using a large plastic bowl and electronic scales that you can reset to zero, weigh out 330ml lukewarm water. Add two ladlesful of vigorous sourdough starter, and stir until the starter is loosely dissolved. Add the flour.

Mix using the handle of a wooden spoon until the mixture comes together. You can now either switch to a plastic bread scraper or use your hands. Continue to mix the dough until it is well amalgamated, scraping the sides of the bowl clean and pushing the scrapings into the mix as you do so. Make a neat round of the dough in the bowl, cover with cling film or a shower cap, and leave in a draught-free place overnight.

The linseeds should be put in a small bowl and barely covered with boiling water. This, too, should be covered with plastic wrap and left overnight.

In the morning the dough should be risen and puffy. Put the now cold linseeds into the dough, add the salt, and mix well to incorporate. This mixing should be thorough but gentle; you don't want to bash the life out of the dough. At this stage I put the dough back into the bowl for a further half hour to relax.

Prepare your tins if using. This quantity of flour needs two 450g loaf tins. Lightly oil them and then dust with flour, banging them on the work surface to get rid of any excess.

Take your dough and either weigh it into two portions or divide by eye. On a floured surface, shape your loaves by gently pulling one edge of the dough away from the mass and folding it over itself, then rotate the dough a quarter turn and repeat, gently pulling and folding, continuing until you have a neat rectangle. At this stage, with your hands at either end of the rectangle, put your thumbs into the middle and, using your fingers, gently pull the dough over your thumbs. You are aiming to make a stout cylinder shape. The goal is to create a little surface tension on the top surface of the loaf, which helps it maintain an even rise in the oven. When the roll of dough is the right shape, gently place it into the prepared tin, seam-side down.

Put the tins somewhere they won't be disturbed, place a tea towel or dish cloth over them, and cover with a sheet of plastic. The plastic envelopes that catalogues come in are useful here. Cut them open lengthwise and lay them over the tea towel or dish cloth.

Leave your loaves alone now until they are well risen and ready to bake. The back of a finger gently pressed into one corner of the dough should create an indentation that very gently springs back. This is the sign that they are ready to go in the oven. Don't let them over-prove and "mushroom" over the tops of the tins.

Slash the tops of the loaves and place in the preheated oven. Splash a little water in the baking tray at the bottom of the oven and close the door. After 10 minutes, splash in a little more water and reduce the oven temperature to 220°C/425°F/ Gas Mark 7.
The loaves are cooked when their tops are nicely browned, and when turned out of the tins and tapped beneath they should vibrate and sound hollow. If they are getting too brown on top, place a sheet of greaseproof paper or baking parchment over them while still in the oven. The loaves need to cool out of the tins on a rack so that air can circulate.

You don't need to make this loaf in a tin, it can be free form, though a little extra care needs to taken with the moulding and shaping, and then the dough can be put into a mould. I often use little enamel pie tins, which have been lined with half a linen tea towel or dish cloth, generously dusted with flour. The loaf should be put in seam-side up, then covered with a tea towel or dish cloth, and plastic. When ready to bake, prepare a small baking tray by dusting the underside with a little semolina. Gently turn your loaf onto the baking tray, slash the top and quickly slide it into the oven onto a hot baking stone, giving the baking tray a sharp outwards tug so the loaf slides off. Cover with a hot saucepan and bake. No water is needed in this case as the steam from the loaf can't escape from the saucepan, and you should get a good oven spring.

Focaccia with Red Grapes and Fennel Seeds

This recipe is for an almost "no knead" focaccia that has a long overnight fermentation in a fridge. Richard Bertinet's basic olive dough recipe was my starting point, but this bread is made with a rye sourdough starter instead of fresh yeast. The topping was in part inspired by Bethesda Bakers, but uses sea salt instead of sugar; and in part by Daniel Leader's recipe for Tuscan Harvest Bread but, unlike his bread, it does not include rosemary.

The combination of the oily, salty bread teamed with the sweet grapes and the burst of aniseed from the fennel seeds is simply magic.

It is a superb bread to make in quantity for parties and other feasts as it is a very forgiving dough. The stretch and fold technique, with periods of allowing the dough to rest, lends itself to making in bulk. Just mix up several different batches and each mix can be resting while you are stretching and folding the next bowlful. The last time I did this I used a total of 3kg flour and produced enough focaccia for a generous buffet for 100. The actual labour for this was not more than about 30 minutes – cutting the grapes in half probably took longer than making the dough! The bread can be made as a tray bake or in individual rounds.

500g stoneground white bread flour
20g semolina (the sort you use for puddings)
175g vigorous rye sourdough starter (approximately one ladleful)
15g salt
300ml tepid water
50ml extra virgin olive oil
100g seedless red grapes
Fennel seeds to taste

Maldon sea salt for the topping
2tbsp extra olive oil for drizzling

Mix the flour, semolina, sourdough starter, and salt together in a bowl. When all ingredients have come together in a sticky mass, add the olive oil and knead gently until the oil has been taken up by the dough.

Lightly oil a clean bowl and, using a flexible bread scraper, scrape the dough into it. Gently form into a loose ball, cover with plastic wrap, and leave for half an hour.

Leaving the dough in the bowl, lift the edge of the dough that is farthest from you. Gently stretch it and then fold it towards you over the rest of the dough. Rotate the bowl a quarter turn, and do the same with the next edge of the dough. Keep rotating the bowl, stretching and folding the dough until it has all been folded and stretched. With practice this will only take a few moments. Cover the dough again, and leave for half an hour.

Repeat this stretching and folding technique another three times. The dough will noticeably change its character as you do this, and should be a cohesive mass by the time you've finished. Cover the dough again, and put into a fridge overnight.

In the morning take the dough out of the fridge and allow it to come up to room temperature. Give it a final stretch and fold, and then turn it out of the bowl onto a lightly oiled worktop and divide it into two even pieces. Gently shape each piece into a round, trying not to expel all the air, then cover and allow to rest for 10 minutes. Lightly flatten each round and place onto an oiled baking tray. Cover and leave to prove for 1 hour.

Gently poke your fingers into the top of each of the now risen discs, pushing outwards so that the disc of dough flattens and expands sideways. Drizzle a tablespoon of olive oil evenly over the dimpled surface of each disc.

Halve the grapes and arrange them, cut side down, on the top of the dough, pushing them gently into the surface. Sprinkle with fennel seeds to taste – I use about a tablespoon for each focaccia – and sprinkle a little coarse Maldon or other sea salt evenly over the top.

Set the oven to 230°C/450°F/Gas Mark 8.

Cover the focaccia again and allow them to have a final rest and prove while the oven is heating up.

Bake for 15-20 minutes, until the bread is risen and pale golden. The tops of the grapes will blacken slightly.

When cooked, take them out of the oven, put on cooling racks, and drizzle a final tablespoon of olive oil over the hot bread.

This bread is delicious while still warm, but don't eat it straight out of the oven as the grapes retain their heat. It is equally good cold and freezes quite well, although the grapes look a bit miserable when defrosted. Because of this, the defrosted focaccia could do with a refresh in a hot oven for a few minutes, longer if refreshing it from frozen.

Alternative toppings include rosemary, either chopped into the dough or tiny sprigs stuck in the surface; orange zest and cumin seeds sprinkled on top; black or green olives; sun-dried tomatoes; caramelised onions – all sprinkled with olive oil and sea salt. Any topping, in fact, that will complement the oily bread. Don't overdo the topping, though, or you risk turning your focaccia into a very doughy pizza!

Wholemeal or Wholewheat Sourdough

A rustic boule made with a high percentage of wholemeal flour, this bread is the genuine staff of life. Full of flavour, dense, chewy, and with a rich, crunchy crust – it is truly bread like our ancestors used to make.

The added bran in the wholemeal flour absorbs a lot of water so this is quite a wet dough, which undergoes a long soaking period. This extra soaking allows the sharp edges of the bran to soften and helps the subsequent rise. However, a brown loaf will never be as light or airy as one made with white flour alone.

This recipe makes one big free-form loaf or two small tin loaves.

700g wholemeal or wholewheat flour
300g stoneground white flour
200g rye sourdough starter
800g tepid water
20g salt

The evening before you want to bake, mix the sourdough starter with the tepid water and stir gently until it is dispersed. Add the flours and the salt, then mix well. Cover the bowl and allow a period of autolyse of about half an hour.

Take the dough and give it a series of stretches and folds. Make sure the inside of the bowl is clean, cover the bowl with cling film or plastic wrap, and leave in a cool place overnight.

The next morning you should find that the dough is light and puffy and ready to shape. Carefully turn it out of the bowl onto a lightly oiled worktop. Either cut into two even pieces or make one loaf. Gently stretch and fold until you have a neat round parcel. Turn the dough so that the seam of the fold is underneath, and shape the boule by using the flat edge of one hand to tighten the shape while you gently rotate the dough with the other hand. You should find the smooth upper surface develops a tight, drum-like appearance.

Prepare a round basket or mould by lining it with a cloth dusted with rye flour. Gently place the round of dough into the mould, seam-side up. If necessary pinch the seam gently together, then dust the surface with a little more flour, fold the excess cloth over the surface, and leave in a draught-free place to prove. A sheet of plastic over the top will help prevent a skin forming.

The dough will take between 2-6 hours to prove. Test it periodically with the back of a finger to see when it is ready to bake. A dent will spring back quickly while the bread is still proving, becoming slower as it reaches optimum proof.

Your oven should be preheated to a hot setting, 200°C/400°F/ Gas Mark 6. If using a Dutch oven or a baking stone, these should also be preheated. Don't forget to put an empty baking tray in the bottom of the oven if you are baking your loaf uncovered.

For baking a free-form loaf in a Dutch oven:

Take out your preheated Dutch oven and remove its lid. Gently tip the dough out of its mould onto your hand and carefully lay it, seam-side down, in the bottom of the Dutch oven. Take a knife and slash the top of the loaf in the pattern your prefer – be careful, it is very easy to burn yourself on the sides of the very hot pan. Quickly place the lid back on the pan and pop it back in the oven. After 20 minutes, remove the lid of the Dutch oven to allow the now well-risen loaf to continue cooking and brown the crust. After another 15-20 minutes test the loaf for doneness by tapping it underneath, listening for the hollow sound and feeling the vibration of a done loaf. Either place it on a wire rack to cool or, if more time is needed, return it to the oven until done. If the crust is getting too brown, cover the loaf with baking parchment.

For baking a free-form loaf on a stone under a pan:

Preheat your baking stone and a large inverted saucepan on top of it. Generously dust the underside of a baking sheet with semolina. Carefully un-mould your dough, seam-side down, onto the edge of the baking sheet. Slash the top of the dough in your preferred pattern. Open the oven and, using a glove, lift the nearest edge of the very hot pan. With the other hand place the edge of the baking sheet with the dough on it in the position you want the bread in the oven. Tilt the nearest edge of the baking sheet up a little and give a sharp jerk back towards you. The dough should slip sweetly off the baking sheet and sit on the baking stone. Carefully lower the hot saucepan back down over the dough, making sure you don't squash its edges, then shut the oven door. After 20 minutes, check the bread. If it is well risen, remove the saucepan to allow the bread to continue cooking. After another 15-20 minutes, test the loaf for doneness by tapping it underneath, listening for the hollow sound and feeling the vibration of a done loaf. If cooked, put it on a wire rack to cool. If more time is needed, return it to the oven until done.

Allow this loaf to cool on a wire rack for at least an hour. This is one of the sourdoughs that likes to sing as it cools.

Sourdough Baguettes

The true French baguette is a long thin loaf with a light but crunchy crust. My version is slightly different, partly because the long thin baguette won't fit into a domestic oven so it is of necessity a shorter loaf; and, in part, because it is made with a rye sourdough starter, giving it a rich flavour. Traditional baguettes are made with a lot of steam in the oven, which results in a light, open crumb. This is almost impossible to replicate in a domestic oven but my recipe will give you a baguette-like loaf that is full of flavour.

The dough is quite wet and so a little difficult to handle, but with practice this will become easier. It is possible to buy special baguette trays in which you prove and bake the loaves. However, you can use a linen cloth or "couche" to help shape and prove the dough. If you use this method, you will also need a bakers peel or an inverted baking tray to get the dough into the oven where it is cooked on a baking stone; or you can transfer the proved dough to another baking tray and cook the loaves on that.

The dough is made using a two-stage overnight process. Some flour, water, and the starter are mixed together in the evening, making a "sponge" or "poolish." The following morning the rest of the flour is added, together with salt, and the bread is made.

This recipe will make four small skinny baguettes or two larger, fatter ones.

425g stoneground white flour
265ml tepid water
175g rye sourdough starter (one large ladleful)
5g fine sea salt

Using an electronic scale that you can reset to zero, weigh out the tepid water. Return the scale to zero and add the rye sourdough starter. Mix gently to disperse the starter in the water. Reset the scale to zero again and add 225g of the flour. Stir thoroughly, clean the insides of the bowl or decant the mix into a clean bowl, cover with plastic and leave overnight. This sloppy mix may start working straight away and you will see the first small holes and craters in the surface even as you are covering it.

The next morning you will see that the surface of your sloppy mix has bubbles all over it, a sure sign that the yeast is multiplying. Add the remaining flour to the mix, put in the salt, and mix thoroughly. This stage is quite hard work as the poolish is often reluctant to take all the extra flour. However, persevere for a couple of minutes and the mix will come roughly together. At this stage, scrape down the insides of the bowl, cover it, and leave it for 10-30 minutes. This short period of autolyse will allow the new flour to start absorbing the liquid in the mix and make it easier to complete the mixing process.

Uncover the bowl and, using the plastic bread scraper or your hand, follow the stretch and fold technique outlined earlier. Stretch and fold the contents of the bowl for two full rotations, or eight stretches and folds. Again scrape the inside of the bowl clean and cover with cling film.

Repeat this stretch and fold at half-hourly intervals for two hours, four times in total. You don't need eight stretches and folds each time though, four will be enough. You will notice that each time you turn the dough it is transforming its character, becoming more dough-like.

Half an hour after the fourth turning, gently ease the now puffy dough onto a lightly floured work surface. Using a steel dough knife or a palette knife, divide into either two or four evenly sized pieces of dough. Stretch and fold each piece into a rectangle. Taking each of your rectangles in turn, fold the long edge in towards the middle of the dough and tightly roll it up into a cylinder. Pinch the dough to close the seam and allow to rest for about 10 minutes. If you are finding the dough too sticky to handle then use a little more flour on your hands and on the work surface. Drape a clean tea towel over the dough while it is resting. After this brief rest, take each roll of dough in turn and, using the flat surface of both hands, roll the dough into an even cylinder of a length to fit onto your baking sheet. At this point you may need to use a little extra flour on the work surface to encourage the dough to roll up and not stick to the worktop. Don't use too much flour, however, or the dough won't roll at all and you may find yourself having to moisten the work surface a little to regain the surface tension. Throughout all this rolling and shaping, treat your dough gently as you don't want to expel all the air.

Take another clean tea towel and dust it with rye flour. This is your "couche," or the linen cloth that will hold your dough while it is proving. Take a rolling pin and lift one of the short edges of the cloth over it. Place the cylinder of dough on the cloth next to the rolling pin and gently lift the two long edges of the cloth so that you create a fold of cloth next to the dough. The dough is now supported on one side by the cloth-covered rolling pin and on the other side by a fold of cloth. You can now place the second dough cylinder alongside the first one. Do this with the remaining two pieces of dough and support the final edge of the cloth with another rolling pin, if you have one. If not, then just roll the edge of the cloth a little to stop the dough rolling off. This all sounds much more complicated than it is to do! The cloth is simply to keep the dough baguettes from touching each other, and to allow them to expand upwards rather than sideways. If you arrange the whole thing on a baking sheet then you can move the proving dough into a draught-free place. Cover the proving baguettes with a tea towel and a sheet of plastic to prove. If you are using a special baguette proving and baking tray, then grease and flour the tray before placing your cylinders of dough into them. Cover with a cloth and a plastic sheet and allow to prove.

The dough will take between 2-6 hours to prove. Test it periodically with the back of a finger to see when it is ready to bake. A dent will spring back quickly while the bread is still proving, becoming slower as it reaches optimum proof.

Your oven should be preheated to a very hot setting, 240°C/ 475°F/Gas Mark 9. If you have made free-form loaves using a couche or cloth, you will need to bake the baguettes on a preheated baking stone. A baking tray in the bottom of the oven will allow you to introduce some steam to help with the rise.

To get your baguettes into the oven you need a rimless or inverted baking sheet. Dust the long edge of the baking sheet with a little semolina. Place the long edge near the edge of the proving couche and, using the cloth to help you, gently roll the proved dough onto the baking sheet. Make five slightly overlapping cuts down the length of the baguette, holding your knife or lame at about 45 degrees to the dough. Open the oven and place the edge of the baking tray with the baguette dough on it at the position in the oven you want the dough to bake. Holding the sheet at an angle, pull it sharply back towards you and the baguette should slip onto the baking stone. When all your baguettes are in the oven, pour some water into the baking tray at the bottom and shut the oven door. This added steam helps the dough rise, giving a good "oven spring."

If using a baguette tray, just pop it in the oven after slashing the tops of the loaves. Add the water to the baking tray in the same way. You may want to take the baguettes out of the tins before they are completely cooked and finish them on the oven rack to encourage an all-over crust colour.

The baguettes will take about 20 minutes to cook. As with all bread, they are cooked when the crust is coloured to your liking and the base gives off a hollow vibration when tapped.

Allow the baguettes to cool on a wire rack before eating.

Baguettes freeze very well, although the crust does tend to flake when they are defrosted. Unfortunately baguettes also stale quickly. Not as quickly as the true French baguette, which needs buying twice a day to ensure freshness, but certainly faster than a large loaf of bread. If you find that your baguette has staled then wrap it in a damp tea towel or dish cloth for about 15 minutes and pop it in a hot oven for 5 minutes or so. This will give it a new lease of life and make it almost as good as new – it will need eating quickly though, straight out of the oven.

Sourdough Pizza

A good pizza is a wonderful thing. Once you have the dough you can add the toppings of your choice and have a piping hot pizza in almost the same amount of time it would take to open a box and cook a ready-made pizza. Using a sourdough base adds an extra flavour dimension, taking your pizza to even greater heights.

This dough mix can be made and kept in the fridge for several days. Alternatively, you could make the dough, shape the bases and then freeze them, so you have a ready supply of pizza bases to hand. Just take one from the freezer, add your toppings, and cook in a very hot oven on a baking stone. They will take a couple of minutes longer to cook if made this way, but they will be worth the wait.

This quantity of dough could make as many as 10 small pizza bases, correspondingly less if you are making bigger, or thicker, bases.

500g stoneground white flour
175ml rye starter
240ml water
50ml olive oil
7g, 1 rounded tspn, fine sea salt

Mix all the ingredients until they all come together in a sticky mass. Allow to sit for half an hour then start the stretching and folding technique.

Stretch the dough and fold it over itself every 40 minutes or so for about four hours. You want to achieve at least four folds and stretches and allow the dough plenty of time to ferment.

When you are ready to shape your pizza bases take as much dough as you want. A small 20cm diameter pizza with a thin crust needs about 100g of dough; a plate-sized thin crust pizza of about 24cm diameter needs about 150g. If you like your pizzas with a thick base, scale up the quantity accordingly.

I use a rolling pin to shape my pizzas. I have tried flinging my dough about as it is done by professionals, but this is definitely a slowly acquired skill. My dough either gets holes in it, becomes a very weird shape that won't fit on either a baking tray or a plate, or gets stuck to either ceiling or floor. Much as I would like to whirl the dough round my head and end up with a perfect circle, I have come to realise that, in this instance, I am better off with a non-traditional method and less wasted dough!

So, to shape the pizza base, take the amount of dough you are using and put it on a lightly floured surface. Do one more stretch and fold with at least four rotations, so that you have a neat almost circular parcel with a smooth under surface. Turn the dough piece over so that the smooth surface is on top and, with a rolling pin, gently roll the dough out into a rough circle. If the dough doesn't want to roll out, allow it to relax for 10 minutes under a cloth. Try rolling it again after the period of relaxation and it should stretch more readily. To reach the full size you want, you may need to allow it to relax a couple of times between rollings. Each time the dough will shrink back less. You may need to use extra flour on the worktop and on the rolling pin so that nothing sticks.

When the dough is the size you require, either place it on an oiled baking sheet or on a bakers peel (or the underside of a baking tray) that has been dusted with semolina. Add your toppings, which can be as simple as fresh tomatoes with mozzarella, freshly ground pepper, olive oil and basil, or as exotic as you like. Put the pizza into a very hot oven 220°C/

425°F/Gas Mark 7, for 10 minutes or so until the edge of the crust has bubbled up and the toppings are cooked to your liking. If you have a very hot oven, the pizza may be cooked in as little as 10 minutes. A thick crust pizza will take longer.

If using a peel or baking sheet you will need to have a preheated baking stone in the oven. Slide the pizza off the peel using a sharp backwards tug. You can move the pizzas around on the baking stones once they have been in the oven for a couple of minutes.

If you want to freeze your dough bases then layer them between baking parchment when they are rolled out to the size you want and pop into the freezer. When frozen you can put them into plastic bags, still separated by the parchment, and use them individually from frozen. Depending on the toppings you are using – not all toppings freeze successfully – you can freeze the pizzas after you have baked them and then reheat from frozen.

Pretzels

The classic German pretzel is both chewy and crunchy. Covered with salt crystals and caraway, it is traditionally eaten with sausage and sauerkraut. My sourdough pretzel is not perhaps a true German classic, but it is a delicious bread nonetheless. It can be savoury or sweet, thin and crunchy, or thick and chewy. A pretzel is a little awkward to shape correctly, but the joy of making your own breads is that you needn't be hidebound by traditional shapes. If you find it a fiddle making the traditional shape, why not devise your own and make your pretzels a shape to suit you?

Pretzels are also one of those breads that undergo two separate cooking processes. The proved dough is dipped in boiling water before baking. This can be a little fiddly, but it is worth doing to give the pretzels their lovely smooth surface.

This recipe leaves the dough to prove very slowly in a fridge overnight. This also means that the cold dough is more manageable when it comes to the initial poaching.

170ml water
175g rye starter
600g stoneground white flour
1tbsp malt syrup (you can find this in health food shops or you can substitute a lesser quantity of molasses, about 1tsp).
10g salt
2tbsp baking powder
1 egg
Maldon or rock salt for dusting
Caraway seeds for dusting

Mix the water, starter, flour, malt syrup and salt together, and allow them to sit for 30 minutes to undergo a process of autolyse. Make sure the inside of the bowl has been scraped clean with a dough scraper, and cover the bowl with cling film or a plastic shower cap.

Uncover the bowl and, using the plastic bread scraper or your hand, follow the stretch and fold technique outlined earlier. Stretch and fold the contents of the bowl for two full rotations, eight stretches and folds. Again scrape the inside of the bowl clean and cover with cling film.

Repeat this stretch and fold at half-hourly intervals for two hours, four times in total. You don't need eight stretches and folds each time though, four times will be enough. You will notice that each time you turn the dough it is transforming its character, becoming more dough-like.

Half an hour after the fourth turning, gently ease the now puffy dough onto a lightly floured work surface. Using a steel dough knife or a palette knife, divide it into about 12 evenly sized pieces. If you want to weigh them, they should be a little over 75g each. Gently shape each piece into a short, fat cylinder and leave them to rest, covered, for about 10 minutes.

With a very lightly floured work surface, shape each of the pretzels. Using both hands, roll each cylinder into a long rope of about 38cm. The centre of the rope should be fatter than the ends, which should taper gently down to a point. Using both hands, roll from the centre of the cylinder out towards the ends, using more pressure as you get closer to the ends. If the rope is resistant to rolling then leave it to rest, covered, for another 10 minutes. This should relax it enough to allow you to continue rolling. If you have used too much flour on the worktop it can be very difficult to roll the dough, it slips rather than rolls. It needs to have a little resistance in order to stretch out successfully. A light spray of water, a wipe with a damp cloth, or even rolling the floury surface with some of the rest of the dough may make the surface sticky enough to work effectively.

When you have a long rope, fatter in the middle than at the ends, cross your hands over each other and pick up each end of the rope, the right end with your left hand and the left end with your right hand. Still holding the dough ends, uncross your hands and then cross them again with a different hand on top this time. This will make a twist in the dough. Lift the two ends of the dough up and towards the fat section of the rope, then lay the ends over the fat section of dough just where it begins to taper down. The thin ends should overlap the dough by a little. This creates the classic pretzel shape of a twisted knot with thick and thin areas of dough giving you the different textures of chewy and crunchy when the bread is baked.

Move the shaped pretzel onto a baking sheet lined with baking parchment. When all the pretzels are shaped and on the baking tray – and don't put them too close together, leave room for growth – put the whole baking tray into a plastic bag and allow to prove for about an hour. At this stage the baking trays can be put into the fridge for up to 24 hours.

When you are ready to bake your pretzels, heat the oven to 200°C/400°F/Gas Mark 6.

Prepare a large shallow pan of simmering water and add two tbsp baking powder – watch out for the furious bubbling up when you add the baking powder. You will also need a tray lined with a dry tea towel and a slotted spoon.

Take the pretzels out of the fridge and uncover them. While they are still cold carefully transfer them, one at a time, to the pan of simmering water. By the time you have the second one in the pan it will be time to take the first one out. They only need a few seconds in the water. Using the slotted spoon, carefully remove the pretzel from the water and place on the tea towel to drain. Continue until all the pretzels have been dipped in the simmering water.

Transfer the now sticky pretzels to an oiled baking sheet, leaving at least 5cm between them. Beat the egg with a teaspoon of water and, using a brush, gently cover the pretzels. Sprinkle with sea or rock salt and caraway seeds if you are using them, and place the full tray of pretzels in the hot oven.

The pretzels will only take about 20 minutes to cook. Keep an eye on them as the thin sections bake quicker than the thick sections. You may need to move the baking trays around in the oven to ensure they bake evenly.

When they are cooked, transfer the pretzels to a wire rack to allow them to cool.

I like my pretzels salty and savoury, but if you prefer a sweet mix try adding poppy seeds and orange zest to the dough mix with 50g sugar. In this instance you could give them a sugar wash, a mix of boiled sugar and water, instead of the egg wash. Alternatively, add 50g sugar to the dough mix and then dust the warm pretzels with a cinnamon and sugar blend. These are fantastic eaten warm with a cup of hot chocolate.

Walnut and Raisin Bread

This delicious bread is well worth the expense of its ingredients. It is quite a dense loaf, but the raisins keep it moist and the walnuts provide a rich, nutty flavour. It is wonderful served with cheese, particularly a goats or a blue cheese, and extraordinary toasted with butter and honey.

The basic dough is my standard white sourdough. It is made using a two-stage overnight process. Some flour, water, and the starter are mixed together in the evening, making a "sponge" or "poolish." The following morning the rest of the flour is added, together with salt, honey and, if you are feeling extravagant, a couple of spoonsful of walnut oil. You can happily substitute a mild vegetable oil here but walnut oil does improve the flavour. After the first period of autolyse the dough is enriched with the fruit and nuts. The bread is then shaped, moulded, proved, and baked.

565g stoneground white flour
325ml tepid water
90g rye sourdough starter (a small ladleful)
150g walnut halves
100g raisins
15ml runny honey
15ml walnut or mild vegetable oil
12g fine sea salt

Using an electronic scale that you can reset to zero, weigh out the water. Return the scale to zero and add the sourdough starter. Mix gently to disperse the starter in the water. Return the scales to zero again and add 200g flour. Stir thoroughly, clean the insides of the bowl or decant the mix into a clean bowl, cover with cling film and leave overnight. This sloppy mix may start working straight away, and you will see the first small holes and craters in the surface even as you are covering it.

If you toast the walnuts it will bring out their flavour. Either gently dry fry them in a pan or spread them evenly over a baking tray and toast them in the oven. Watch them closely as they will burn readily. Allow them to cool completely and then put them in a tough plastic bag and bash them about a bit with a rolling pin. This will break them up a little, but not too much. You certainly don't want walnut crumbs.

The next morning you will see that the surface of your sloppy mix has bubbles all over it, a sure sign that the yeast is multiplying. Add the remaining 365g flour, the honey and the oil to the mix, put in the salt and mix thoroughly. This stage is quite hard work as the poolish is often reluctant to take all the extra flour. However, persevere for a couple of minutes and the mix will come roughly together. At this stage, scrape down the insides of the bowl, cover it and leave it for 10-30 minutes. This short period of autolyse will allow the new flour to start absorbing the liquid in the mix and make it easier to complete the mixing process.

Uncover the bowl and add the nuts and the raisins. Using the plastic bread scraper or your hand, follow the stretch and fold technique outlined earlier and stretch and fold the contents of the bowl for two full rotations, eight stretches and folds. The nuts and fruit won't want to be incorporated at this stage, but as you continue the stretch and fold process the dough will take them up. Again scrape the inside of the bowl clean, and cover with cling film or plastic wrap.

Repeat this stretch and fold at half-hourly intervals for two hours, four times in total. You don't need eight stretches and folds this time though, four times will be enough. You will notice that each time you turn the dough it is transforming its character, becoming more dough-like.

Half an hour after the fourth turning gently ease the now puffy dough onto a lightly oiled work surface. This quantity of dough will make two 450g tin loaves or one large free-form loaf. If you are making two loaves, divide the dough at this stage and complete your shaping. Stretch and fold the dough to make a neat shape, either round or rectangular, and then complete your moulding to the shape you prefer. For a round free-form loaf, put the seam-side down and, using the side of your hand, rotate the loaf all the while gently pulling the sides under the base so tightening the surface. For an oval loaf, using your thumbs, roll the dough up into a tight cylinder shape. If the nuts are sticking out of the surface push them back in to the dough with your thumb.

Place the dough in your chosen moulds lined with rye flour-dusted cloths, seam-side up. Pinch the seam closed, dust with a little more rye flour, then gently fold the spare cloth over the top of the dough. Put in a draught-free spot to prove, and cover with a sheet of plastic. Alternatively, put the dough into oiled and floured tins, seam-side down.

The dough will take between 2-6 hours to prove. Test it periodically with the back of a finger to see when it is ready to bake. A dent will spring back quickly while the bread is still proving, becoming slower as it reaches optimum proof.

Your oven should be preheated to a hot setting, 200°C/400°F/Gas Mark 6. If using a Dutch oven or a baking stone, these should also be preheated. Don't forget to put an empty baking tray in the bottom of the oven if you are baking your loaves uncovered or in tins.

For baking a free-form loaf in a Dutch oven:

Take out your preheated Dutch oven and remove its lid. Gently tip the dough out of its mould onto your hand and lay it, seam-side down, in the bottom of the Dutch oven. Take a knife and slash the top of the loaf in the pattern you prefer – be careful, it is very easy to burn yourself on the sides of the very hot pan. Quickly place the lid back on the pan and pop it back in the oven. After 20 minutes remove the lid of the Dutch oven to allow the now well-risen loaf to continue cooking and brown the crust. After another 15-20 minutes test the loaf for doneness by tapping it underneath, listening for the hollow sound and feeling the vibration of a done loaf. If cooked, put it on a wire rack to cool. If more time is needed, return it to the oven until done. Keep a close eye on the tops of the loaves as any nuts that are sticking out of the surface of the loaf could burn. If this does look likely, cover the loaves with baking parchment.

For baking a free-form loaf on a stone under a pan:

Preheat your baking stone and a large inverted pan on top of it. Generously dust the underside of a baking sheet with semolina. Carefully un-mould your dough, seam-side down, onto the edge of the baking sheet. Slash the top of the dough in your preferred pattern. Open the oven and, using a glove, lift the nearest edge of the very hot pan. With the other hand place the edge of the baking sheet with the dough on it in the position you want the bread in the oven. Tilt the nearest edge of the baking sheet up a little and give a sharp jerk back towards you. The dough should slip sweetly off the baking sheet and sit on the baking stone. Carefully lower the hot saucepan back down over the dough, making sure you don't squash its edges, and shut the oven door. After 20 minutes, check the bread. If it is well risen, remove the saucepan to allow the bread to continue cooking. After another 15-20 minutes test the loaf for doneness by tapping it underneath, listening for the hollow sound and feeling the vibration of a done loaf. If cooked put it on a wire rack to cool. If more time is needed, return it to the oven until done.

For baking a loaf in a bread tin:

Place a baking tray in the bottom of your oven and allow it to preheat. When your bread is ready to bake, slash the tops in your preferred pattern and gently place them on the oven rack. Pour a little water into the hot baking tray and quickly shut the oven door. After 10 minutes open the door and pour a little more water into the tray. Shut the door again. Keep an eye on the loaves and after 25-35 minutes test them for doneness. Take a loaf out of the oven and tip it out of the tin, tapping it on the underside. There should be a hollow sound and you may feel a vibration through the loaf. If they need a little longer they can go back in the oven out of the tin, straight onto the oven rack. When cooked they should be removed from the tins, if still in them, and placed on a wire rack to cool.

Prune and Pink Peppercorn Bread

This lovely loaf, inspired by Emmanuel Hajiandreou, is made with half rye and half white flour. The result is a very flavoursome, moist loaf. It doesn't have much rise, because of the rye flour, so has quite a dense crumb structure. It keeps well, improving after a day or so as the flavours develop. Pink peppercorns are more readily available than they used to be. They have a delightful spicy flavour and are a very pretty colour. Rye flour doesn't react well to handling, so this bread has almost no work.

300g light rye flour
400g stoneground white flour
200g rye starter
700ml tepid water
400g prunes, stoned and roughly chopped
12g/2½tsp salt
15g/1tbsp pink peppercorns

2 x 450g loaf tins, well greased

Using an electronic scale that you can reset to zero, weigh out the tepid water. Return the scale to zero and add the rye sourdough starter. Mix gently to disperse the starter in the water. Return the scales to zero and add the white flour. Stir thoroughly, clean the insides of the bowl or decant the mix into a clean bowl, cover with cling film, and leave overnight. This sloppy mix may start working straight away, and you will see the first small holes and craters in the surface even as you are covering it.

The next day add the rye flour, the salt, the chopped fruit, and the peppercorns. Stir thoroughly with a wooden spoon; you will end up with a mixture rather like a sloppy cake dough. Spoon half the sloppy mix into each of the prepared tins. Wet the back of your fingers with cold water and gently smooth the surface of the dough – don't compress it, just smooth it over.

Cover the tins with a tea towel and a sheet of plastic and leave in a draught-free place to prove for 2-4 hours. There will be very little rise but you should see some.

The oven needs to be heated to 220°C/425°F/Gas Mark 7. Put an empty baking tray on the bottom shelf so you can introduce some steam to help the rise.

When the oven is hot and the loaves are ready to bake put them, in their tins, into the oven. Add a little water to the baking tray in the bottom of the oven and shut the door.

Bake the loaves for about 30 minutes, or until they are brown on top and when tipped out of the pan and tapped beneath they sound hollow. This is a very sticky dough, and sometimes the bread is a little reluctant to come out of the loaf tins. If they won't release easily the first time you try it, leave the tins in the oven for five more minutes. This little bit of extra cooking time may make a difference. If the loaves still won't release from the pans but you think they are cooked, leave them to cool for a couple of minutes in their tins. Then carefully take a blunt knife and run it around the inside of the pan, sticking close to the edge and trying not to cut the loaf. This should allow the loaves to be tipped out. I sometimes put the loaves back in the oven for a minute or two after they have come out of their tins, as this allows the bases to dry out a little and take on some colour. Leave the loaves to sit on a wire rack until they are cool.

Breads made with rye flour often taste better the day after baking since the flavours have had time to mature and come together. This bread keeps exceptionally well.

Borodinsky Bread

This fragrant and flavoursome loaf was said to have been invented after the Battle of Borodino in 1812. This may or may not be true but it is certainly a romantic tale; Andrew Whitley relates the story of its inception in his great book Bread Matters.

Borodinsky is rye sourdough flavoured with molasses and coriander seeds. The flavour and texture improves with age, and this wonderful bread complements smoked fish exceedingly well. The combination of the thinly sliced, sweet fragrant bread, sharp horseradish cream, and smoked mackerel is sublime.

Rye flour has almost no gluten in it and so does not respond to handling well. In fact this particular bread is easier to assemble than a cake mix. Just don't expect a good rise – rye on its own makes for a dense loaf.

270g rye sourdough starter
230g light rye flour
30g molasses
90ml warm water
5g/1tsp fine sea salt
5g/1tsp ground coriander
10g/2tsp coriander seeds

1 well-greased small loaf tin (450g)

Start by sprinkling a few of the whole coriander seeds into the bottom of the greased loaf tin.

With the exception of a ½tsp of the remaining coriander seeds, mix all the other ingredients together in a bowl. This will be a very sloppy mix that can almost be beaten with a wooden spoon. However, treat it gently, but make sure to mix it thoroughly. As soon as it is mixed, wet your hands and scoop out the dough mixture and form it into a rough oblong a little smaller than your bread tin. The water will stop the dough sticking to you. Carefully place the oblong of dough into the prepared tin and, re-wetting your hands if necessary, gently smooth the surface of the dough. Sprinkle the reserved coriander seeds evenly over the top of the loaf and gently press them into the surface. Cover the tin with a tea towel or dish cloth and a piece of plastic, and leave it in a warmish place to rise. This dough will never have the spectacular rise of some breads, but when it is ready to bake it should be much bigger than when you put it in the tin.

The oven needs to be heated to 220°C/425°F/Gas Mark 7. Put an empty baking tray on the bottom shelf so you can introduce some steam to help the rise.

When the oven is hot and the loaf is ready to bake, put it into the oven in its tin. Add a little water to the baking tray in the bottom of the oven and shut the door.

Bake the loaf for about 10 minutes ,then reduce the heat to 200°C/400/Gas Mark 6. Cook for another 30 minutes or until it is brown on top and when tipped out of the pan and tapped beneath it sounds hollow. If the bread is browning too fast, cover with baking parchment.

This is a very sticky dough and sometimes is a little reluctant to come out of the tin. If it won't release easily the first time you try it, leave the tin in the oven for five more minutes. This little bit of extra cooking time may make a difference. If the loaf still won't release from the pan but you think it is cooked, leave it to cool for a couple of minutes in the tin. Then carefully take a blunt knife and run it around the inside of the pan, sticking close to the edge and trying not to cut the loaf.

This should allow the loaf to be tipped out. I sometimes put the loaf back in the oven for a minute or two after it has come out of the tin; this allows the bottom to dry out and take on some colour.

Allow the loaf to cool completely before slicing it. If possible leave it for a further 24 hours to allow the flavour to develop.

Sourdough with Mixed Seeds and Spelt

This delicious loaf, which I usually make as a free-form boule, is enriched with a mixture of five different seeds and also has a little spelt flour; this is an ancient variety of wheat with a great nutty flavour. If you can't get hold of spelt you can substitute wholemeal flour instead.

The seeds are soaked before use so that they don't absorb too much moisture from the bread dough. You can make up your own seed mixture using favourites, or use the small bags of ready-mixed seeds from the supermarket. My favourite at the moment has sunflower, poppy, pumpkin, linseed, and sesame seeds in it. I have made variations of this loaf with millet and amaranth seeds, too. Have fun making your own mix.

100g mixed seeds
100ml boiling water
335g stoneground white flour
90g spelt flour
120g rye sourdough starter
200ml tepid water
5g/1tsp salt

Put the seeds in a small bowl and pour the boiling water over them. Cover with cling film or plastic wrap and leave to soak overnight.

On the morning of your baking day, mix the ingredients, including the soaked seeds and their water, together. When it is amalgamated, leave for a period of autolyse for half an hour.

Using the plastic bread scraper or your hand, follow the stretch and fold technique outlined earlier and stretch and fold the contents of the bowl for two full rotations, eight stretches and folds. Scrape the inside of the bowl clean and cover with cling film.

Repeat this stretch and fold at half-hourly intervals for two hours, four times in total. You don't need eight stretches and folds each time though, four times will be enough after the initial eight. You will notice that each time you turn the dough it is transforming its character, becoming more dough-like.

Half an hour after the fourth turning, gently ease the now puffy dough onto a lightly oiled work surface. This quantity of dough will make one large free-form loaf. Stretch and fold the dough to make a neat shape, either round or rectangular, and then complete your moulding to the shape you prefer. For a round free-form loaf, put the seam-side down and using the side of your hand rotate the loaf, all the while gently pulling the sides under the base and thereby tightening the surface. For an oval loaf, using your thumbs, roll the dough up into a tight cylinder shape.

Place the dough, seam-side up, in your chosen mould, which should be lined with a rye flour-dusted cloth. Pinch the seam closed, dust with a little more rye flour, and gently fold the spare cloth over the top of the dough. Put in a draught-free spot to prove, and cover with a sheet of plastic.

The dough will take between 2-6 hours to prove. Test it periodically with the back of a finger to see when it is ready to bake. A dent will spring back quickly while the bread is still proving, becoming slower as it reaches optimum proof.

Your oven should be preheated to a hot setting, 220°C/425°F/Gas Mark 7. If using a Dutch oven or a baking stone, these should also be preheated. Don't forget to put an empty baking tray in the bottom of the oven if you are baking your loaf uncovered.

For baking a free-form loaf in a Dutch oven:

Take out the preheated Dutch oven and remove its lid. Gently tip the dough out of its mould onto your hand and carefully lay it, seam-side down, in the bottom of the Dutch oven. Take a knife and slash the top of the loaf in the pattern you prefer – be careful, it is very easy to burn yourself on the sides of the hot pan. Quickly place the lid back on the pan and pop it back in the oven. After 20 minutes remove the lid of the Dutch oven to allow the now well-risen loaf to continue cooking and brown the crust. After another 15-20 minutes, test the loaf for doneness by tapping it underneath, listening for the hollow sound and feeling the vibration of a done loaf. If cooked, put it on a wire rack to cool. If more time is needed, return it to the oven until done. If the loaf is browning too quickly, cover the surface with baking parchment.

For baking a free-form loaf on a stone under a pan:

Preheat your baking stone and a large inverted pan on top of it. Generously dust the underside of a baking sheet with semolina. Carefully un-mould your dough, seam-side down, onto the edge of the baking sheet. Slash the top of the dough in your preferred pattern. Open the oven and, using a glove, lift the nearest edge of the very hot pan. With the other hand place the edge of the baking sheet with the dough on it in the position you want the bread in the oven. Tilt the nearest edge of the baking sheet up a little and give a sharp jerk back towards you. The dough should slip sweetly off the baking sheet and sit on the baking stone. Carefully lower the hot saucepan back down over the dough, making sure you don't squash its edges, and shut the oven door. After 20 minutes, check the bread. If it is well risen, remove the saucepan to allow the bread to continue cooking. After another 15-20 minutes test the loaf for doneness by tapping it underneath, listening for the hollow sound and feeling the vibration of a done loaf. If cooked, put it on a wire rack to cool. If more time is needed, return it to the oven until done.

If you are baking without a cover you can just slide your loaf onto the baking stone or a preheated baking tray. Use a little water in another preheated baking tray at the bottom of the oven to introduce a little steam.

Allow the loaf to cool completely on a wire rack before cutting.

Crumpets

For the last recipe in this book I thought you might like an idea for something very simple that will help use up all the surplus starter you might otherwise throw away as a discard when you refresh your rye starter.

Crumpets are traditionally eaten in Great Britain as a tea-time treat. They are best enjoyed toasted, preferably with a toasting fork in front of an open fire, and smothered in butter. Some add jam, but traditionalists often sprinkle them with a little salt before eating the crumpets, still hot. The open texture makes a wonderful vehicle to hold all that melted butter!

The amounts given are just a guideline: if you prefer your crumpets sweeter with the "sour" flavour reduced, use freshly refreshed starter after it has had a couple of hours to start working, and use more or less sugar according to your palette. The amount of salt is also to your taste as crumpets can be treated as a sweet or savoury snack. Don't overdo the baking powder, though, as it can leave quite a strong and distinctive taste. It is wise to sieve the baking powder before you add it to the mix, as little lumps are often slow to dissolve. Make just enough mix up at a time to use quickly. If you want more crumpets make a further mix immediately before you want to cook them.

The crumpets are cooked in rings, since it is a very sloppy mix, on a griddle or in a frying pan. They shouldn't be too thick, about 1.5cm, otherwise the centre can still be undercooked when the bottom is done.

270g sourdough starter, either recently refreshed or the discard from a refreshment
1-2tsp sugar

1tsp salt
½tsp baking powder

Thoroughly grease the interior of the crumpet rings, and put them in a lightly greased frying pan or griddle over a moderate heat.

Put the sourdough starter into a clean bowl and whisk in the sugar and salt. If the starter is a little thick, add a small amount of water; it should be a thick, dropping, consistency.

When your pan and the crumpet rings are hot, add the sieved baking powder to the mixture. It should start to bubble up very quickly. Using a ladle, pour some mix into the centre of your hot crumpet rings. Don't make them too thick. Allow to cook gently for about 4-5 minutes. You will see holes appearing on the upper surface of the crumpets. Don't rush them!

When the crumpets are nearly cooked they will start to shrink away from the edges of the metal rings. Using a cloth to protect your hands, try and get the ring to release the nearly cooked crumpet. Turn it over and cook the top for a minute or two. The base should be a uniform golden brown colour, and the top should just be lightly coloured.

Allow the crumpets to cool on a wire rack, and toast them before eating.

These freeze well and can be toasted from frozen – layer them with parchment before freezing so you can separate them later.

References

Bacheldre Mill

Bertinet, Richard

Bethesda Bakers:

Doves Farm

Leader, Daniel

Panary: Paul Merry.

Real Bread Campaign

Shipton Mill

Smashwords E books from Independent Authors

Tolkien, Ed

Whitley, Andrew. 2009, Bread Matters: Why and how to make your own. Fourth Estate, London

Glossary:

Autolyse: A process of allowing flour to absorb water and start the process of conversion into dough

Boule: A round, free-form, loaf

Couche: A mould made out of floured cloth for baguettes, or other slender loaves.

Gluten: The protein in flour which allows the bread to rise

Knock Back: To expel the air from partially risen bread dough – not used in this method

Lame: A bakers blade on a handle – used for slashing the tops of unbaked loaves

Mother: The sourdough starter or culture

Peel: A long-handled flat wooden or metal board used for putting bread dough into and taking bread out of ovens.

Poolish: A dough pre-mix of flour, water and yeast, or flour, starter and water. Often the first stage in slow fermentation.

Prove: The process of allowing dough to rise

Sponge: A dough pre-mix of flour, water and yeast, or flour, starter and water. Often the first stage in slow fermentation.

Terroir: A French term indicating the flavour of place

Wholemeal Flour: in America, this is known as wholewheat

Acknowledgments

Thanks are due to Tim and Eleanor Osborne for inspiring me to have a go. To Paul Merry at Panary, who showed me I could bake for a living, Bethesda Bakers for encouragement and inspiration, and to all at Marshfield Country Market for liking my bread. To Lucy Mennell, who acted as guinea pig and recipe tester, and to Lisa Cussans for her careful editing. And, of course, to Ed Tolkien for his cover design.

Also by Victoria Osborne: Non-Fiction titles in The Curious Peasant Series

Tagines

Bantams in the Garden

For news of forthcoming titles, published at monthly intervals, visit www.thecuriouspeasant.co.uk

About the Author

Victoria Osborne is a true born-again peasant. She has worked at a wide variety of jobs over the years, including riding teacher; deck hand on a traditional three-masted schooner; school registrar; curtain-maker; business manager; and specialist antique dealer. She has now turned her hand to telling others about the skills she has picked up over the years. Victoria has experimented with self sufficiency, living on a smallholding in Wiltshire where she has kept chickens, bees, rabbits, quail, sheep, pigs, horses and, most recently, a working donkey. She grows her own vegetables, cures and smokes her own bacon and ham, joints her own venison, and makes bread both for sale and for her family's consumption. She has made wine, baskets, soap, preserves, and built a replica Iron Age roundhouse, as well as a coracle. Victoria has most recently been a research student at a West Country university, studying for a PhD in Artisan cheesemakers, only giving this up when the natural curiosity of the peasant finally took over!

Visit her website at www.thecuriouspeasant.co.uk

Did you like this book?

Thank you for buying this book. I hope you enjoyed it and that you have tried making your own sourdough starter and sourdough breads. If you enjoyed reading it perhaps you would take a moment to leave a review on Amazon. Your positive feedback helps me to continue writing books in The Curious Peasant series.

Thank you!

Victoria Osborne

Made in the USA
Coppell, TX
31 August 2023